SOMEONE IS MISSING AT DINNER
Copyright © 2025 Tricia and Tom Hack

All rights reserved. Neither this publication nor any part of this publication may be reproduced or transmitted in any form or by any means, electronic or mechanical, including photocopying, recording or any information storage and retrieval system, without permission in writing from the author.

Aspects of this story have been fictionalized. Names, characters, places and incidents either are the product of the author's imagination or are used fictitiously, and any resemblance to actual persons, living or dead, businesses, companies, events, or locales is entirely coincidental.

Scriptures taken from the Holy Bible, New International Version®, NIV®. Copyright © 1973, 1978, 1984, 2011 by Biblica, Inc.™ Used by permission of Zondervan. All rights reserved worldwide. www.zondervan.com The "NIV" and "New International Version" are trademarks registered in the United States Patent and Trademark Office by Biblica, Inc.™

Print ISBN: 978-1-4866-2704-2
eBook ISBN: 978-1-4866-2705-9

Word Alive Press
119 De Baets Street, Winnipeg, MB R2J 3R9
www.wordalivepress.ca

To our children and grandchildren:
may you know and experience the enormous love of God
and the fullness of His presence in your lives
as you daily seek to live for Him.

I love my family. We get together almost every Sunday and have dinner. We play games and take walks. Best of all, Grandma makes yummy dinners!

But now someone is missing at dinner: my Uncle David. He no longer comes because he died. We miss him very much.

When Uncle David came to our dinners, he liked to play jokes on Grandpa and make me laugh. He also told stories about his four crazy cats, like when they all tried to sleep on his bed and he woke up with a tail in his mouth.

Grandma misses Uncle David's bright smile and big hugs. She puts a candle on the table to remember him because he was like a light shining God's love to others.

Grandma says that we can be like a light shining God's love to others, just like Uncle David did.

Grandpa loves to sing and play songs about God. I like it when he sings. He even sings when he is sad and misses Uncle David.

Grandpa says that singing about God's love and power helps us trust God even when we don't know why sad things happen.

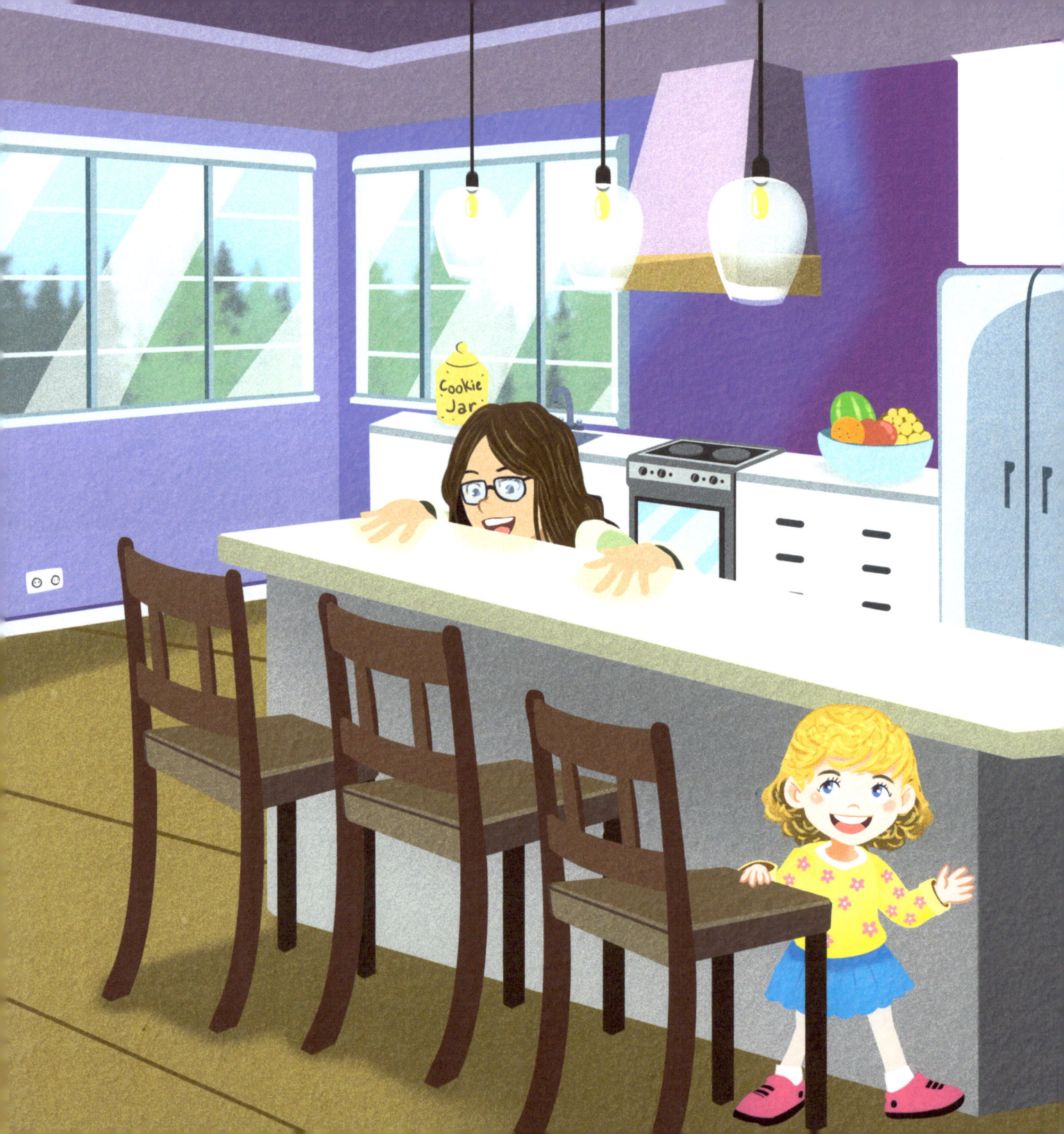

Uncle David was married to my Auntie Tay. She reads stories and plays hide-and-seek with me. Mommy says that when Auntie Tay plays hide-and-seek, it reminds us of how Uncle David liked to play.

There are times when Auntie Tay is sad, like at Christmas dinner. My mommy is a really good storyteller. She talks about Uncle David and shows videos of him from her phone. This helps Auntie Tay and everyone remember and laugh about the funny things Uncle David used to do.

When Daddy prays to thank God for the food, he also thanks God for Uncle David. My daddy and Uncle David were good friends. They both liked to build and fix things. Daddy helped him fix up his house.

At dinner, they sometimes did silly things and got in trouble from Grandma. But Grandma wasn't really upset. I saw her smiling from the kitchen.

My Auntie Becca is Mommy's sister. She and her husband, Uncle Jordan, have a little baby boy and a crazy dog. Uncle David liked to play with the dog and get him so excited that he would run all over the house. We all laughed and called it the zoomies.

Auntie Becca and Uncle Jordan made a special photo book about Uncle David's life, starting when he was a baby. Every so often, we look at the book. It helps us to remember how special Uncle David was.

My great-gran is Grandma's mom and she comes for dinner too. Great-gran is wise and a good listener. She always knows the right thing to say at the right time.

Great-gran says that it's good to come together even when we feel sad and miss Uncle David because being together is like a bandage that helps to heal our hurt.

When Mommy feels sad, we go to the cemetery. The cemetery is a big grassy field with stones that have people's names on them, and lots of pretty flowers. It is a place where we remember people who have died.

Sometimes Mommy talks to God. Sometimes she is quiet. At other times, she laughs and tells me about Uncle David when he was little. She also thinks about Uncle David in heaven. Mommy says these are some ways of remembering Uncle David that help her when she is missing him.

I like to pick dandelions and put them on Uncle David's stone. Mommy says that Uncle David would like that.

There are times that I miss Uncle David and cry. I wish we could play at the park, dress up my cat, and eat macaroni and cheese together. Mommy says that it's okay to cry when I need to. She says it helps to share our feelings when we are sad.

When you miss someone who has died, it is like a puzzle with a lost piece. You can still make the puzzle and see the beautiful picture, but there will always be a piece missing.

When we are missing someone, it shows how much we love them.

Although we miss Uncle David, what helps the most is to know that he is with Jesus in heaven. He is no longer sick or in pain.

One of Uncle David's favourite Bible verses was John 3:16, which says,

"For God so loved the world that he gave his one and only Son, that whoever believes in him shall not perish but have eternal life."

Uncle David believed that God loves us and sent His Son, Jesus, to become one of us, to teach us, and most importantly to save us by dying for our sins. Sins are things we choose to do that God doesn't want us to do. Our sins keep us from being in a close, forever friendship with God.

Mommy says that because Jesus was perfect and never sinned, He could do what we couldn't. He took the punishment for our sins by dying on the cross for us. He died so we can be forgiven.

But Jesus did not stay dead. He did something amazing and came back to life! He defeated death and made the way for us to have an everlasting relationship with God.

When we tell Jesus we are sorry for our sins, believe that He died and came back to life to save us, and ask Him to be our Saviour, we begin a forever friendship with Him. We also become part of God's family.

Uncle David isn't at our family dinners anymore. But Grandpa says one day we will be with him again at the biggest and best party ever! The Bible calls the party the Wedding Supper (Revelation 19:9).

It will be a feast of happiness where we celebrate that Jesus won over sin and death, and we live with Him forever without sadness, sickness, or pain.

At this wonderful celebration, all of God's family will sing, praise, and thank Jesus for all the great things he has done.

We look forward to the day when we will be with Jesus and Uncle David in heaven. When that day comes, we will give Uncle David a great big hug.

For now, we are thankful for the beautiful memories we have of Uncle David and God's promise to be with us in both sad and happy times.

We pray that our story and the hope Jesus gives us will help your family when you are missing someone special at your family dinners.

www.ingramcontent.com/pod-product-compliance
Lightning Source LLC
LaVergne TN
LVHW071029070426
835507LV00002B/86